An Eyeful of Earth, An Eyeful of Ocean

Also by Mandana Zandian

Blue Gaze (Negah-e Abi), 2002

The Labyrinth of Silence (Hezartu-ye Sokut), 2004

Tree in my Heart (Dar Qalb-e man Derakhtist), 2009

An Eyeful of Earth, an Eyeful of Ocean
(Chashmi Khak, Chashmi Darya), 2012

Re-reading the Ten Nights
(Bazkhani-ye Dah Shab), 2014

An Eyeful of Earth, An Eyeful of Ocean

Selected Love Poems of Mandana Zandian

Translated from the Persian
by
Ahmad Karimi-Hakkak

Ibex Publishers,
Bethesda, Maryland

An Eyeful of Earth, An Eyeful of Ocean
Selected Love Poems of Mandana Zandian (1999-2014)
Translated from the Persian by Ahmad Karimi-Hakkak

Cover illustration courtesy of Majid Zandian

ISBN: 978-1-58814-133-0

Copyright © 2014 Mandana Zandian
Translation copyright © 2014 Ahmad Karimi-Hakkak

All rights reserved. No part of this book may be reproduced or retransmitted in any manner whatsoever, except in the form of a review, without permission from the publisher.

Manufactured in the United States of America

The paper used in this book meets the minimum requirements of the American National Standard for Information Services—Permanence of Paper for Printed Library Materials, ANSI Z39.48–1984

Ibex Publishers strives to create books which are as complete and free of errors as possible. Please help us with future editions by reporting any errors or suggestions for improvement to the address below, or corrections@ibexpub.com

Ibex Publishers, Inc.
Post Office Box 30087
Bethesda, Maryland 20824
Telephone: 301–718–8188
Facsimile: 301–907–8707
www.ibexpublishers.com

Library of Congress Cataloging-in-Publication Data

Zandiyan, Mandana, 1971 or 1972-
[Poems. Selections. English]
An eyeful of earth, an eyeful of ocean : selected love poems / by Mandana Zandian (1999-2014) ; translated from the Persian by Ahmad Karimi-Hakkak.
   pages cm
 1. Zandiyan, Mandana, 1972—Translations into English. 2. Love poetry, Persian.   3. Persian poetry—Translations into English.   I. Karimi-Hakkak, Ahmad, translator.   II. Title.
PK6562.36.A53A2 2014
891'.5514—dc23   2014028653

Contents

Translator's Introduction 9
Blue Gaze 15
   Moment of Union 17
   Fragrance of Love 19
The Labyrinth of Silence 21
   Green 23
   Love 25
   The Sound of Silence 27
   Gray 29
   Loneliness 30
The State of Red 33
   Fantasy 35
   Fall 37
Tree in My Heart 39
   One 41
   Four 42
   Five 43
   Six 44
   Seven 45
   Eight 46
   Nine 47
   Eleven 48
   Twelve 49
   Fourteen 50
   Eighteen 52
   Nineteen 53
   Twenty 54
   Twenty-One 55

Twenty-Two 56
Twenty-Three 57
Twenty-Four 58
Twenty-Eight 59
Thirty 60
An Eyeful of Earth, An Eyeful of Ocean 61
One 63
Four 64
Six 65
Seven 66
Nine 67
Eleven 68
Twelve 69
Thirteen 70
Fourteen 71
Seventeen 72
Nineteen 73
Twenty-Two 74
Twenty-Three 75
Twenty-Five 76
Twenty-Seven 77
Twenty-Eight 78
Twenty-Nine 79
Thirty 80
Thirty-Two 81
Thirty-Three 82
Thirty-Five 83
Thirty-Six 84
Thirty-Seven 85
Thirty-Eight 86

Thirty-Nine 87
Forty 88
Forty-Two 89
Forty-Three 90
Forty-Five 91
Forty-Six 92
Unpublished Poems 93
He was Sitting There 95
Rain Writes Like You 96
A Phantom Sits Between Us 97
In Me 98
We are Left Alone No More 99
The Silhouette and the Eyes 100
I Can No Longer Be Contained 101
Words are Alive 102
I Bare My Chest 103
There was No Dawn 104
I Pass Over My Own Surface 105

Translator's Introduction

Mandana Zandian is an Iranian-American poet, journalist, and physician, and all these aspects of her life seem to have played a part in the character of the poetic universe she has created over the past fifteen years. That much at least is known to those who read her poetry in the original Persian, the language that she loves beyond rhyme or reason and that she uses deftly in her compositions. Few people outside her immediate linguistic and cultural community, however, are familiar with her poetry, a fact that has instigated the effort here in the hope that her work may find its place in a wider world; this book, in other words, aims at making available to the reader an impressive lyrical impulse and an expression of deep-seated emotions, most centrally love, that enliven the human soul.

At its core, Zandian's poetry articulates love in all its dizzyingly diverse faces and facets, including carnal desire, as a most solid foundation for human relations, a fundamental assumption that shines eloquently through her poetry. In articulating this desire, Zandian treads subtly and in uncannily sophisticated abstractions, giving rise to an aesthetic that ultimately aims at the creation not only of beauty and of mutuality in relations that connect love and caring, man and nature, the worlds within and outside us. In that connection, she also sees healing as a basic function of all relationships based on love. What completes her depiction of mutual loving and caring as intimately intertwined is the broadest, most widely cast, canvas of nature and its grandest of assets. The earth with all the trees that stand erect upon it and the wind that kisses and caresses them ceaselessly, on the one hand, and the ocean with all the waters that flow from it or run toward it and into it seem to stand in awe as two individual human beings, whole and wholly together, gaze at a single horizon or pointing to it with singular purpose. All this provides a solid ground for contemplation of the part that humans can and must play, not just as lovers, but as citizens of a world of infinite diversity and beauty, of utter calm and unfathomable depth.

What makes the earth and the ocean such fitting figures for vast and deep love also turns them into both the model for living lovingly and peacefully and the highest reward for doing so. Ultimately, their grandeur and glory are most essential to all efforts at the creation of beauty. In Zandian's poetry, we often see the lyrical I at the center of the poem in the act of soothing the object of her affection, which often occupies the position of her addressee, particularly when he is absent. Contemplating such scenes, whether knowingly or intuitively, moves us to an idea of the mutual and loving complementarity of peace and beauty, most universally understood, most intimately experienced. In her poetic world, the grandest manifestations of the world bear witness to the grandeur of love, whether through a speaker waving to an approaching or departing addressee or through caressing explorations of hands or lips as they move over a lover's body. In all this, Zandian's lover is ennobled through gestures and gestations of love in all its senses.

Born in Esfahan, Iran, in 1972, Mandana Zandian went through her education in her homeland, graduating from Shahid Beheshti University's School of Medicine in 1997. She has lived through the tumult and various tribulations of Iran's recent history, the revolution and the violence it ushered in as well as the devastating war between Iran and Iraq in the 1980s, have colored her childhood, while an incomplete and badly thwarted reform movement has left an indelible mark on her youthful psyche. When she and her husband ultimately moved to the United States in 2000, she launched her career in medical research, keeping her involvement with the affairs of her homeland on the margins of her career as a scientist. Meanwhile, poetry was gaining ground steadily in her imagination, and the first two collections of her poems, *Blue Gaze* (2002) and *The Labyrinth of Silence* (2004) were published in Iran. In exile, it was the mentorship of a distinguished figure in the community of expatriate Iranians that catapulted Zandian to a professional plane in journalism. Beginning in 2006, the late Iraj Gorgin detected and nurtured the talent in the young woman as a public intellectual, one in the use of the Persian language and the art of the interview. By then, Gorgin had been an icon of radio and television journalism both in Iran and in the expatriate Iranian-American community for nearly fifty years, and his mentorship gradually pushed Zandian to a level of professionalism that could no longer be assigned to life's margins. Over the past seven years or so, she has produced two books primarily based on conversations and conducted numerous in-depth interviews with various luminaries among Iranians in exile. In more recent years, through the art of radio interviews, she has further extended her reach into the life and work of Iranian and Persian-speaking poets like herself all over the world, as well as in her home country of Iran.

These events, and doubtless her exposure to various contexts of her personal and social life, have also moved Zandian forward in demonstrable ways, and her poetry testifies to this impressive expansion eloquently, even though this aspect of her work may have only a pale reflection in translation. In other words, Zandian has moved steadily toward wider and vaster arenas for her conceptualization and expression of love as the centerpiece of human existence. In her later compositions, one rarely comes across love as a domesticated feeling bound by blood relations or sanctioned by social institutions; rather, all that is left in a great many of her poems is a speaker and an addressee in naked mutual gaze, one speaking lovingly, the other absorbing love as if it were mother's milk for the soul, nurturing it, nourishing it, and being ennobled by it. In fact, we may venture to say that the figures stand in mutual contemplation of something vast and nameless within them, around them and between them—something that no language, no attempt at understanding can reach: that, in a word, is what Zandian's poetry calls love and celebrates in all its manifestations. This book can only hope to offer a faint, distant glimpse of it.

Blue Gaze

(1999-2002)

Moment of Union

On the dust-heap of moments
settles the memory of the beloved's sincerity.
the tingling of the sun arrives
I know it—it's the sound of his footsteps.

Warm streams of tender feelings
pour into the ocean of my heart
it's time for union in the recesses of my mind
when once again the heart puts the lips to the cup.

The silver cloud of love's passion
sets up its tent over the breadth of my words
colorful arches of his excited glances
spread canopies over my senses.

Thunder rises in the depth of my heart
in the cocoon of the beloved's virginal memories
its lightning rods fanciful calls to silence
this is his remembrance incarnate—yes, yes!

Interminable intimacy
springtime in the beloved's chamber
spread your wings up over the horizon
rain forever upon this twosome of faith.

Out of the beloved's desire
rises a fulsome spirit yielding to his need
love becomes worship all over:
keep him in your embrace, God!

Fragrance of Love

It was night, your scent lurked in my chest
the music of your bluest words,
and the tingling of your silence
filled the desert of my heart
              with God's footsteps
and put my soul aflame with the desire to sing …

You were filled with the will to give
and I was drowning in desire,
how softly you held my heart's hand
and led me to the stillest silence
to where the night was so blissful
and the heart's blue words found their target.

Fearless, I broached the words in my heart
along a rosary of faith
and cast it whole over the noon of night
and you made a graft between me and it …

Many a night, in the privacy of the heart
you have led me to the chamber of your divinity
lifted me up to the world of fantasy
elevated me to a canary's song
              to the ascension of the dove.
You have raised me to the climax of God's sublime
   silence!

Sheltered by you
I rubbed off the dust of utter exhaustion
was filled to the brim with memories of you
and shared your glance with the poppies
and the night was blissful …

And I heard the footsteps of your memories
in the chamber of my words
and the tingling of the silence
you had planted in me echoed.

And now forever
I seek to repeat that immensity
and forever
I will sing this mystery for you:
you are the most exquisite faith
and I adore the longing to come together with you:
look toward me, my love
                         my most intimate love.
See me behind this constant longing.

The Labyrinth of Silence

(2002-2004)

Green

Your love
is the most unsung of my poems.

Your caresses
are moonlight's velvet,
your kisses
apple blossoms.

My silence
leans on your glance
and my impatience
rests in your silence.

Your smile
is an eternal trust
and your embrace
the only land
where I do not get lost.

My poem
believes in you,
you who were
the earth of its second growth
and of its original sin.

Your presence
Wipes away my isolation:
see the shoots of my desire
they have spread a green carpet
along this path
to welcome you.

Love

I rose up …
I rose up and shook your heart's hand.

The scent of your glance
spreads over my soul's faith.

The blue of your feelings
has seeped into the heart of my paper,
and your green accent
has spoken
of a new season.

The breeze danced
and a drop of light
kissed my poem's throat.

I inhaled the look of your words
and believed in the depth of your faith
and my earth turned the color of the sky …

I raised a hand
to open up the highest of your sky's windows
I wanted to see beyond your blues as well
beyond your unreachable blues …
how far away was that reach!

This side of me
there were clouds and an anticipation,
that side of you
The moon and the stars and rain.

I drank the music of your rain
my pen pranced
and the pulse of my words turned blue.

My glance knotted in your crimson horizon
how much patience was there
and how much constancy—
and silence.

I heard the sound of light
turned back
and the horizon was filled with the dawn
and you pulsated through the heart of every minute.

I looked at you
you looked at me
and there was a basket of red apples …
and a pond of clear tears.

The Sound of Silence

I was looking
at the green bliss
that was in your eyes
at that boundless smile
and the rising of the rain in the sky of your heart.

What a tender affair is the crying of the heart—
how endless …

Spring was singing
behind all windows
and the swallows and the acacias
and the hills, rivers, the breeze.

How replete I was with the need, the desire
for the songs of your heart
and you were still silent,
still peaceful.

What were you waiting for?
the rising of a scream?
incarnation of a miracle?
or the crystal shine in a teardrop?

How heavy for my heart
your marine indigo quiet
how filled with implications …

And in the mirror I saw a hard lump
blocking your love's throat as mine
and the mirror spoke—and broke:
and you, ah,
forever silent.

I looked
at the tenderness of your lump
your familiar eyes
the color of your smile.

How came it that I could not hear the sound of your
    patience
as it was pouring poetry
on all these moments?

What was I expecting?
the lightning of a roar
the shattering heart of a lump?
and a downpour of tears?

Your blessed smile
was the spirit of a song and a poem
and your eyes
defenders of your silences:
what a tender affair
how boundless …

Gray

I stared
at screams yielding
to the color of silence,
at hearts lending an ear
at all yieldings,
at all this graying despair
at all the disbelief lurking in us.

How was the story of the sea and the little fish
lost to all memories
amid the hubbub for a loaf of bread?
How did the pain of the journey
exhaustion of the road traveled
cover up in dust all our longing for the destination?

How we were left behind
in the friction of our movement toward laughter.

I am thinking:
how would it be possible already
to bear witness
to the denial of our existence?

Loneliness

Losing yourself
in an ocean's nest
and grasping the feeling of thirst
from memory, not breaking,
abandoning yourself to love
in the desire for a glance,
making a bridge to yourself
within the fortress of silence.

Sprouting again
blossoming
shooting forth
growing again, to the fullest.

Putting baskets full of budding light
in the hands of your days
as would the fountain of the sun
and passing by with no regret—lips shut.

Bearing the silence of songs in patience
anticipating as much as the warm desert air
saying nothing but nothing
tuning your heart to nothing!

Living like mirrors, without color, without sound,
speaking nothing but of the friend
not breaking yourself
free, frank, fleeting
heavenly blue
flying to the edge
returning to yourself.

The State of Red

(2004-2006)

Fantasy

The sky turns red
the sun of your lips
descends over my shoulders
and you settle on my breasts.

I get wet
you get wet
and the skies stretch.

The curves of my body
step over the boundaries of yours
a rainstorm of kisses rattles our shoulders
your body's scent multiplies in my throat
I quiver
I crack
I spill over
"Ah, love!" …
I whirl …
………………
… the hollow of your not being there scratches my
 glance.
I break
I shatter
the night crumbles
dawn passes by the window:
"The blue of your face is not there."

What a red dream! ...

Traces of your fingertips
pass over the curves of my thoughts
beyond which moment are you?

How I am myself!
I ennoble the earth
and had no fear of God
when picking the fruit.
Yet, with you
and for your sake only
I hailed fear,
because my dreams
had turned your color,
because my hands
fell short
of the murmurings of your fingertips,
because every little thing
filled me with the thoughts of you,
because your hands
Had gone way beyond my destiny,
because the moon will never kiss
the sun's lips,
because that's how love is.

Fall

A thousand words had been left unsaid
a thousand pathways not taken
to present a thousand pretexts for you
to stay ....
....
* * *

As if a stranger
I cannot move beyond your departure.

I have tried it over a thousand autumns:
$$\text{impossible.}$$

Tree in My Heart

(2006-2009)

One

You moved by lightly
and the tiled garden sipped the light.

Life was beauty let loose.

And a tree grew tall in every tile
and the trees
complimented one another on your stroll.

I bent over your hands
and your smile wafted over my face
a lotus grew
and water
blessed the calm in your voice.

The moment was an eternity
and the windows of the world
murmured the songs of meandering mirrors.

Four

You are so true
as to awaken my dreams.

I am too much in love for the patience of the earth
come let us pullulate.
homesickness is perhaps a winter
in anticipation of a momentary spring.

Five

Your glance does not waft over me
so I can be one with myself.

I bare your memory and the desert's spirit
cracks up
over the hollow of my poem.

Six

In the beginning was the word
and the word was exile:
they had fitted the moccasins of exile
perfectly for our feet,
so we took to the road
and became exiles.

We were twins with the spring
we were words and turned into notes
and exile was the bed of our love songs
we made love and we became the lyrics.

In the end there was nothing
there was the word
and the word was the voice
and the truth was a vast circle
flowing over the edges of our bed
dissolving in a luminous glance.

Seven

Love makes us:
I believed in you
and my heart was created.

Eight

You poured the ocean in my glance
and said:
skies are the land of flying.

Inside the shell of your memories
my homesickness is turning into a pearl.

Nine

I am standing tall
in celestial ports
waving of my hands
for the joy of your arrival,
which wades about in the liquid brown of my eyes.

Intense anticipation gathers pace
turns into a song of nakedness
it is a dazed moment
pulsating through my breathing
in tandem
with the booty of your kisses.

The sun speaks in your local dialect,
and my carnal desire grows oceanic
pulling me
all the way
along the lines of love's palms
through the woods of your chest
to the farthest nocturnal shore.

Eleven

If you had not held my hand
how would I learn
that one can smile
even in the absence of the sun?

When your voice rains upon me
even a single drop of the moon
falling in my bowl of water
would be enough:
I will turn into light.

Twelve

Like rain
you proffer and you turn into the sea.

Like the sea
I abandon myself and I rain.

Light is but the shadow of our nakedness.

Fourteen

Windows of the world were shut
wind blew from an uncertain direction
and light was a miracle
that would not happen.

You were sitting face to face with pain
so I could stand on my own shoulders
and offer your voice a green apple.

And your voice
was the nest of memories.

We were without a pathway, without a voice
and the sense of our being
was nothing but losing our way in the day's environs.

We lit seven sticks of candle
and circled
the seven ceremonial grains of wild rue
around the seven stars, that polished your voice.

But pain was not capable of reading the heart's hand
and we knew
that if we opened our mouths
a downpour would descend.

Only when the seven cypresses bent over the water
you could utter the word trees in such green cadence
that the seven windows of flight
would open toward the seven skies.

Your wide open smile
spreads the scent of the seven token foods
on the Nowruz table.

"Windows of the world are shut
                                      no longer".

Eighteen

You strip away the green garment
and murmur my body's bearings.

I conquer you—and myself besides
and am lost in both worlds.

I have become a woman
exiled by your manly presence—

And history will record
the naked whirling of my lips
around the crimson music of your body.

Nineteen

Like a gypsy woman
I am looking for pathways with no destination
in the nooks of your embrace.

I feel a craving for the sea
and the humidity of your shoulders
and the waves of your body
that have turned native in mine.

You are gone
and the sunflowers at the edges of my skirt
have grown as tall
as the southernmost of God's dreams.

Twenty

We drown ourselves in each other's dreams
and wakefulness is born.

Twenty-One

Love is liberation
and your embrace
the homeland I've never had.

Twenty-Two

It is the seventh day of spring
the moon glides over our glimpse's forehead
and the sea submerges in our embrace.

Twenty-Three

Happiness was a secret
that your smile
revealed to life.

Twenty-Four

You surge in my fancy
the word's bosom is a thing of beauty.

Twenty-Eight

Your hands knew it:
Man's fate
Is the world's fate.

Spring is an extension of your smile.

Thirty

Leaving means not getting there
staying means not being:

only you are the perfect presence.

An Eyeful of Earth, An Eyeful of Ocean

(2009-2011)

One

Love
is the song of the world's waters
the color of flight in the moon's imagination
the scent of the sea in the air of a tile
and the tree, forever alone
and time
forever now.

Four

An eyeful of earth
an eyeful of ocean.

I was a little bird
and one night
I flew away from the fantasies of gods
so you can hold me in an embrace as free
as the sky holds a wandering star.

Six

Perhaps no words had remained
except water, which
brooding over all those gardens,
would not go down any throat, when
our hands felt wet
and our bodies
turned into monuments of a miracle
that love had handpicked
from the fabric of the ocean.

Seven

I was a shadow
a sketch mingled with the noon of the night
who flapped a wing
over the dust of its voice
so the sky of your eyes
should renew itself with fantasies of flying.

Then time blew along the length of your form
and love,
more delicate than a sketch of the moon
would not sink
in the oceans of your palms.

Nine

Look into the rose-garden of your palms
so pain
will move away
along with the breeze that blows from the remotest corners
of your glance.

Life is a smile
sprouting through the springtime of your voice,
and time
a pause
that gods have stolen away
from the vast sorrowland of love.

Eleven

Time
is a shapeless casement
opening onto an unknowable dream,
that blows your hands
through the eyes of gloom
to transform the lunar etching
along the sky's forehead
into the sun.

Twelve

You blink there
and my eyes bare themselves here
like water turning into a cloud
in my palms
cross veins and cars
to come cover your hands noisily,
like a leaf
that would not leave a palm tree
nor move in seasons,
or in pain, away from the ocean
that is the bluest dream of the goldfish
in your chest.

My surest certitude:
you pulsate rain there,
and here
eyelids of the night
grow red craving your chest
growing heavy.

Thirteen

You move away
and my shadow stretches along the length of your absence
longer steps
more passable pathways
closer us
and the revelation of the secret between the earth and the bird:
there lives a sunrise in the bosom of every shadow.

Fourteen

As you happen
night turns into poetry
the moon rises full
and I turn into
a necklace
on the lookout of your memory.

Call me
I want to pluck pomegranates from the palm of your hand.

Seventeen

Love is a naked secret:
moon's reflection
in the river that is us.

Nineteen

Like a pomegranate
you have spilled over the autumnal cup
so the tree's hands can be aflame
and a grape's glance
can turn into wine
amid the patience in your eyes.

Your gaze is a bird
lifting the earth
up to different skies.

And your smile is the sun
that rises from the night's chest
and spreads all over me—all the way.

Twenty-Two

I have been through the pyre many times
like the moon in the sea
and every time
a green butterfly
has spread my ashes over the umbra.

Half phoenix
half heron
I have been the moon of my own gloom.

Twenty-Three

Your voice
is a river
which, over the curves of its pebble-stones
the moon turns into wine
and night is a circle whose meandering corners
form the shape of a bird
on the shoulders of the willow
along the path of your fingers
there is a lyric for tree and for water
whose body parts
breathe in your chest
so the jagged sun would not injure the earth's song.

Twenty-Five

Where upon my non-being
should I plant your not being there
so the pomegranate tree
a living ghost in the season of your birth
will not feel dazed
upon the golden waterfall of this autumn …

Twenty-Seven

I know your not being line by line
not seeing you passage by passage
and the turns of you glance
that laughs out a thousand words
so a moment of you
should breathe through
this half-chipped moon
and this night should live on.

Twenty-Eight

Evenings come my way without your name
and your not-being
no longer fills the void of your empty place.
I wish you had turned off the lantern of the moon
so I would not see the night.

Twenty-Nine

Anticipating your hands
summer waves its hands
before the court of your fantasy
in all the gardens
of red roses,
and, as they arrive, your hands
turn the tree's glance into fruit
on the branches of your voice,
ornaments of rain,
color of pomegranate,
peeling
the night
anticipating your fantasy
in all the gardens.

Thirty

I learned the flowing from the river
and the returning from the rain
so I can forever come back to you.

Thirty-Two

Far or near
sprout anywhere in my life you wish.

Your voice is a mirror
where your hands multiply
and flying
is a secret
that, searching for a page of your voice,
connects
lights and birds together.

Thirty-Three

Your hands resemble a chandelier of a thousand flames
growing in the rain
so a butterfly's fancies
would not burn
amid the dark clouds.

Nakedness is a wound
a cypress
lingering on the body of the fall,
an ocean
scratching
the heaven's voice.

… And along the lines of your hands
butterflies
turn into kisses.

Thirty-Five

I kiss the letters of your name
the vineyard turns red.

Thirty-Six

Every time I uttered
your name to a river
it turned into an ocean:
a mirror
for me to drown myself in.

Thirty-Seven

Between darkness and light
lies the illusion of a single leaf
that the notes of your voice
have murmured
over the earth's veins,
silence
is water's music
and love
a thicket
grown over the reverberations of your solitude.

Thirty-Eight

Except the heaven of your mouth
no ocean
turns into the sun
over this night,
and this rain
which locks my lips
onto your eyelids
as if in a rhyme,
is one with the sun—and yet
your hands
exceed
the sunflower that is my throat.

Do not shut your eyes:
I am born, not repeated, in you.

Thirty-Nine

There is a garden in me
for your hands
for your sorrow
and your joy,
and the averting of your eyes,
signs of the sun's nobility,
in the midst of a storm.

A bird for your flight
in a meandering sky
and a river for the ocean that you are.

There's a secret in me
that you have redeemed from these waters
naked.

Forty

Naked
as night,
a stranger, resembling yourself only,
you have spilled over the life of your hands
so the eyes of this garden
should light up
on a distant fantasy
of shades of green.

Rivers
have always been pregnant with babes of leaves.

Forty-Two

I am thinking of you
and, like springtime,
love
throws light
out of balance:

I blow within you
you rain upon me
and night becomes one with day.

Forty-Three

To watch you
I bequeath a moon to the sky
and darkness to the earth.

Butterflies kiss your shoulders
your hands capture the scent of poetry
waters reiterate your frame
you smile
and the night sinks.

Forty-Five

Lonelier than a night
that knows it is pregnant with the purest of morns
you and I flow in each other's embrace
much like the earliest glance of the gods
upon the birth of the sun.

Love, ancient and diehard,
discovers us
and joy
supersedes a tough pain.

Death is the secret
revealed to humans only
to make life eternal.

Forty-Six

You do not leave my fancy
and the redness of fire is no match for me.
Listen
this is the color of my chiaroscuro
in modulating your silence.

Unpublished Poems

(2011- 2014)

He was Sitting There

He was sitting there—
water drinking
the gurgles of his voice gulp upon gulp
through the turn at one end of a straw
made of a branch of the Tuba Tree.

A thousand windows were alight
and the road
was an arrival
that an iteration of his hands
tied to the mirror's wings
and light
resembled its own seclusion
and a recurrence
of birds
flew off from Simorgh's nest.

Rain Writes Like You

Rain writes like you
walking over the shadows
gingerly
as the moon
gains luster amid the migration of cranes
like reams of the water
that seeps
in the folds of the lines,
that turns the remotest slumber of the rock
into flowers.

The tree
is the earth's soul,
poetry
the loudest
of human silences;
and your hands form a pathway
that plants
particles of dust
through patches
of light.

A Phantom Sits Between Us

A phantom sits between us and
we blow eye to eye and
the breeze charts the outline of our forms,
colorless, it glides through our hands and
pecks at our eyes and
a thousands red apples
fall to the ground
from the folds of former figures.

Put on these fig leaves and one night
let loose your dreams on the veranda of my eyelids:
we cross us over
and marine nymphs
sketch arabesque patters and
the earth overhears us.

In Me

In me
nameless women
pluck your passage
from the season's branches.

You pass over my edges
I do not,
and our eyes, formless, frolic with our hands
my hands blush
as they watch you
and life turns into a wound that will not tire
of mouthing beauty and no name.

We are Left Alone No More

We are left alone no more.
We are away, our eyes run loose on the shoulders
    of the horizon
        weightless, and
the hands of your absence
blow over the skin of mine without a word, and
our bodies blossom,
rain picks up
like lines of not seeing you
in thoughts that
to this day
run free over the shadows of our hands
through a book, through the daily paper, and
on the balcony of your smiles.

It is as if time would stand and we would pass by,
we would pass and time would stand by,
and life should start sprinkling our eyes behind our
    words, and
we return and come together beyond wounds
that open up to themselves only,
not even seeing us.

The Silhouette and the Eyes

Between a silhouette that is emptied of light
and the eyes freed from night
lies the distance of a mirror.

In the oblivion of storms
clay gods
fall apart, and
through the slumber of trees
cold seasons turn into the sun.

Our earth is the altar of luminous memories
that catch on fire
amid reams of gloom
and learn the garden
through their eyes
in the flight of a single bird.

I Can No Longer Be Contained

I can no longer be contained
in the confines of a pen case
or the tale a river tells
as it twists its tongue in the ears of words,
stretching my hands over my shadow
so the night
can read the day in Brail.

I push the drapes aside,
the winds and the seasons I push aside,
time melts on the mirror's naked limbs
and doubles the image of these hands' sweet destruction
that is mimicked in the lines of my shadow
that sinks into my fingers
and pulls me out
of the doubtless pits of this land
that can be contained neither in the confines of a pen case
nor in the river's tale.

Words are Alive

Words are alive:
they breathe
they dream
they make love and,
like pain, grapple death's waist and
give up ghost and
become poems and
live on.

We are not alone,
we are wandering birds
who are never stunned
out of our dream of words.

I Bare My Chest

I bare my chest
the moon is whole
your voice rises in my throat:
— "Love is twins with death"
Your roots speak to the water
and the seagulls' song
is let loose
on the shore's chest.

We have plucked our eyes from trees
and there is seven skies of mirrors
between our hands and the heavens.
— "death
     always
         grows in the midst of light."
The vases by the window know this
and we do, we who have guessed
at the hand that the wave holds and
who rise free from the earth's bosom.

Like the moon, blowing through all her halves
like love, which is twins with loneliness
and like you, twins with water:
bathe me beyond our hands
and adorn me with a memory
that is the brightest harbor in the whole world.

There was No Dawn

There was no dawn.
I threw my hands up in an air well
and turned into a cloud.

The mesa blasted through my fingers
and a set of lost eyes
receded
behind my eyelids.

I
was extinguishing
in a fire that was me
and a mirage filled with fish
was digging its way
up to the gullet
of the well's coverings

I Pass Over My Own Surface

I pass over my own surface
do not sink in myself like soil
that softens under the weight of the world's waters
and sprouts in the pathway's fancy.
For the tribal gypsies of this frame
the pathway is a snapshot of the passing:
Through the night they climb down my shoulders
and my shadow, who always gets wind of this before myself,
throws herself down the window
in the midst of the noise
and, like the wind, takes my hand,
sheds its shell
at the tip of every branch,
and at the threshold of its own abstraction
sprouts at your fingertips.

Made in the USA
Charleston, SC
21 September 2014